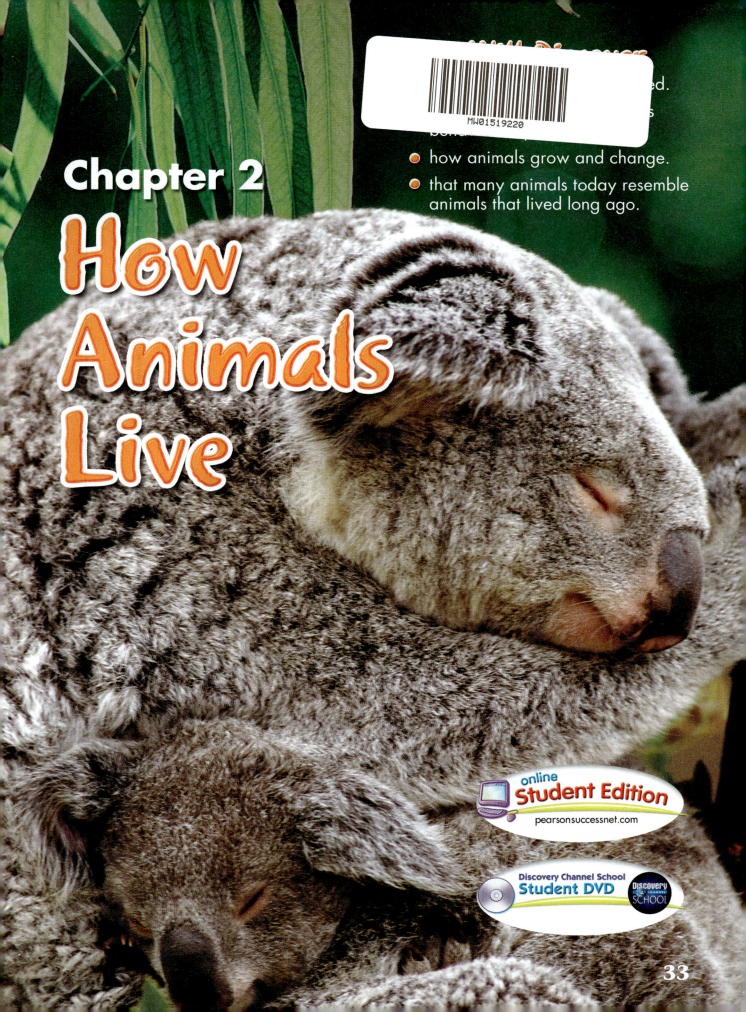

Chapter 2

How Animals Live

- how animals grow and change.
- that many animals today resemble animals that lived long ago.

online
Student Edition
pearsonsuccessnet.com

Discovery Channel School
Student DVD

How do different animals live, grow, and change?

vertebrate

trait

inherited

migrate

34

hibernate

adaptation

larva

pupa

Directed Inquiry

Explore How can you make a model of a backbone?

Materials

pipe cleaner

10 pieces of wagon wheel pasta

9 soft fruit jelly rings

What to Do

1 **Make a model** of a backbone. Bend the end of a pipe cleaner into a knot. String a piece of wagon wheel pasta on the pipe cleaner so the pasta rests on the knot. Next string a jelly ring.

2 Add another wheel and a ring. Keep going until you have used 10 wheels and 9 rings.

3 Bend the other end of the pipe cleaner. Make a knot to hold everything on. Can you bend your model backbone?

Process Skills

Making and using a model can help you understand scientific ideas.

Explain Your Results

How is your **model** different from a real backbone? How is your model like a real backbone?

How to Read Science

Reading Skills

Sequence

Sequence is the order in which events take place. Clue words such as *first, next, then,* and *finally* can help you figure out the **sequence** of events. They are marked on the museum display card.

Museum Display Card

Sea Jelly

A sea jelly grows up in stages. First, an adult makes young called larvae. Next, each larva becomes attached to a rock. Then, each larva grows and becomes a polyp. Finally, each polyp grows into a group of young adults.

Apply It!

Make a graphic organizer as a **model** to show the life cycle of the sea jelly. Write each of the four events in the life cycle after your four clue words.

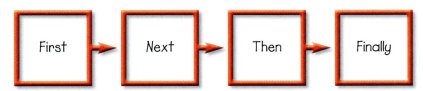

First → Next → Then → Finally

It's early morning in the forest and the birds are singing. You look down at your feet and notice ants marching by. You stand very still, listening and watching. Suddenly, you spot what looks like two dogs walking through a grassy field in the distance. As you focus your eyes you realize they are not dogs. You've spotted a wolf and her pup! Animals come in many shapes and sizes. Even though they may be different, do animals need the same basic things to live?

AudioText

Lesson 1

How are animals grouped?

All animals have the same basic needs. Animals might be grouped by how they look, where they live, or how they act.

What All Animals Need

Nearly all animals need water, oxygen, food, and shelter to live. Animals can get water from drinking or from the foods they eat. All animals also need the gas oxygen. They get oxygen from the air or from water. Most animals that live on land have lungs to breathe in oxygen. Many animals that live in water, such as fish, breathe with gills.

Animals also need food and shelter. They get their food by eating plants or other animals. Shelters protect animals from the weather and from other animals. While some animals build or seek shelters, others use their own hard shells as their homes.

Needs of Animals

Water	Oxygen	Food	Shelter

1. ✓ **Checkpoint** What do all animals need?

2. **Writing in Science** **Descriptive** In your **science journal,** write about how your favorite animal meets its basic needs.

Ways of Grouping Animals

How we group animals depends on what we want to learn about them. Animals can be grouped by where they live or how they act. They also may be grouped by how they look. A body feature passed on to an animal from its parents is called a **trait.** Traits can include things an animal does.

One animal can be placed into different groups. For example, a group of animals that eat mice can include snakes, hawks, and owls. A group of animals that fly can include hawks and owls, but not snakes.

Animals with Backbones

Another way to group animals is by whether or not they have a backbone. An animal with a backbone is called a **vertebrate.** Cats, birds, fish, and snakes all have backbones and other bones in their bodies. Their bones grow as the animals grow. Their bones give them strong support. This allows many vertebrates, such as elephants, to grow very big.

This lynx is a vertebrate.

Groups of Vertebrates

Fish
These vertebrates spend their entire lives in fresh water, ocean water, or both. Most fish have slippery scales and breathe through gills.

Amphibians
Frogs, toads, and salamanders belong to a group called amphibians. Many amphibians spend part of their lives in water and part on land. Most young amphibians live in water. They get oxygen through gills and through their smooth, moist skin. As they grow, most amphibians develop lungs that they use to breathe air.

Reptiles
Snakes, lizards, turtles, crocodiles, and alligators are reptiles. They mostly have dry, scaly skin. These vertebrates breathe air through lungs.

Birds
Birds are vertebrates with feathers and bills that do not have teeth. They breathe air through lungs. Wings and light bones help most birds fly. Their coats of feathers help them stay warm.

Mammals
The vertebrates that you probably know best are called mammals. Mammals have hair at least during part of their lives. The hair keeps them warm. Mammals breathe air through lungs and feed milk to their young.

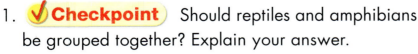

1. ✔**Checkpoint** Should reptiles and amphibians be grouped together? Explain your answer.

2. **Art** in Science Think about two animals that share some of the same traits. Draw a picture of each animal "in action" using a shared trait.

Animals Without Backbones

Most animals do not have skeletons made of bones inside their bodies. These are the animals without backbones, or invertebrates. Sea stars, butterflies, and spiders are some invertebrates. There are many more kinds of invertebrates than vertebrates, as the chart shows.

A soft sac filled with liquid supports worms and sea jellies. A hard shell supports clams. Insects and other arthropods have a hard covering on the outside of their bodies. These kinds of structures cannot support very big animals. Most invertebrates do not grow as big as most vertebrates.

Many invertebrates are very small. Several million tiny roundworms may live in one square meter of soil. You may not notice many invertebrates, but they live all over Earth.

Kinds of Animals

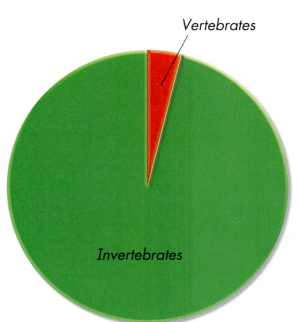

The whole circle stands for all kinds of animals. The small piece shows that kinds of vertebrates are only a small part of the total.

Kinds of Invertebrate Animals

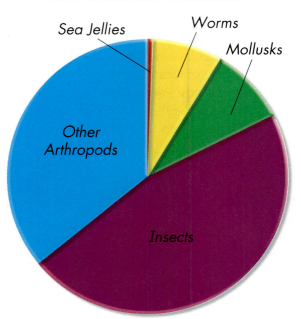

Most kinds of invertebrates are insects.

This dragonfly is an invertebrate.

Major Kinds of Invertebrate Animals

Sea Jellies	Sea jellies have soft bodies and long, stinging body parts. The body of a sea jelly is made mostly of water. A sea jelly uses its stingers to stun its prey before pulling it into its stomach. Most sea jellies live in the ocean.	
Worms	Worms are animals with long, soft bodies and no legs. You've probably seen an earthworm in the soil. These invertebrates help keep soil healthy.	
Mollusks	Mollusks are animals with soft bodies. Some mollusks include the octopus, squid, clam, and snail. Many mollusks have a hard shell.	
Arthropods	These animals are members of the largest group of invertebrates. They wear their skeletons outside their bodies. The bodies of arthropods are made up of more than one main part and they have legs with joints. Insects, spiders, and crabs are all arthropods.	

✓ Lesson Checkpoint

1. If a rattlesnake and a black widow spider both make poison, why are they put in different groups?

2. Explain why most invertebrates are small in size compared to most vertebrates.

3. **Math in Science** There are 5 vertebrates in someone's backyard. There are 20 times as many invertebrates as vertebrates there, too. How many invertebrates are there?

How do animals grow and change?

Different animals have their young in different ways. But all animals grow and change during their life cycle.

Life Cycles

An animal's life starts out as an egg. Sometimes the egg develops into a young animal inside the mother. Then the mother gives birth to a live young. For other animals, the mother lays an egg outside of her body. Then the young develops in the egg and hatches when it is ready.

When some animals hatch or are born, they look like their parents. Many other animals change a lot before they look anything like their parents.

Adult butterflies lay eggs.

 Egg
This is a close-up view of a very small egg. The picture has been magnified, or made to look bigger.

Life Cycle Stages	
Birth	Animals are born or hatch.
Growth	Animals get bigger.
Development	Animals change into adults.
Reproduction	Animals produce young.
Death	Animals' lives come to an end.

4 Butterfly
The adult butterfly comes out of the chrysalis.

3 Pupa
Inside a hard covering, the larva's body changes.

2 Larva
The butterfly larva is called a caterpillar.

A Butterfly's Life Cycle

The egg is the first state in the butterfly's life cycle. The tiny egg is hard to see.

A caterpillar hatches from the egg. It is now a **larva.** The larva must eat a lot to survive. It starts munching on the plant where it lives.

The larva grows. It sheds its skin several times. Then the larva spins a covering around itself. A hard covering, or chrysalis, forms. The larva is now called a **pupa.**

The larva's body begins to change when it becomes a pupa. It grows wings and jointed legs. It begins to look like an adult butterfly. Soon it breaks out of the chrysalis. The adult butterfly dries its wings and flies away. After laying eggs, the butterly dies. Its life cycle is complete.

1. **✔Checkpoint** What is the purpose of the pupa?

2. **Sequence** List the sequence of steps in a butterfly's life cycle. Use the signal words *first, next, then,* and *finally.*

Some Vertebrate Life Cycles

Vertebrates have different kinds of life cycles. Some vertebrates, like frogs, go through many changes as they grow and mature. Other vertebrates, like pandas or monkeys, do not change as much.

A Frog's Life Cycle

Just like insects, many amphibians change quite a lot as they become adults. Did you know, for instance, that a very young frog looks and acts a lot like a fish?

Look at how a frog changes during its life cycle. This frog completes all the stages of its life cycle in one summer. All frogs do not develop in the same way. In colder places, a developing frog may dig into the mud during the winter. It will not become an adult frog until the following spring or summer.

A panda cub gets a gentle nudge.

A Mammal's Life Cycle

Unlike amphibians and insects, young mammals do not change very much as they become adults. Many mammals look like their parents when they are born. Like you, they grow as they get older.

Most mammals develop inside their mother's bodies. When they are born, the babies drink milk from their mothers. They also have hair or fur.

It will be many years before you become an adult. A young rabbit, however, is ready to leave its nest and live on its own when it is less than three weeks old. It will be an adult at about six months.

Even though it's very small, a new-born panda pup has the same body form and the same number of legs as its parents.

Frog Life Cycle

② Tadpole
Tadpoles hatch from the frog eggs. Tadpoles live underwater and breathe with gills.

① Eggs
Mother frogs often lay hundreds or thousands of eggs in the water.

③ Growing Tadpole
As the tadpole grows, it starts to change. Its tail becomes shorter. Legs begin to grow. The back legs grow first.

Before a tadpole becomes an adult frog, it has to grow lungs so it can breathe on land.

④ Adult Frog
The adult frog lives on land and in the water. It will need to return to the water to lay its eggs.

✓Lesson Checkpoint

1. Before a frog can live on land, how must its body change?

2. How is a mammal's life cycle different from a frog's or a butterfly's life cycle?

3. **Writing in Science** **Expository** Think about how mammals care for their young. In your **science journal,** describe why this kind of care might be helpful for most mammals.

How do adaptations help animals?

Animals have special body parts, features, and ways of doing things that help them survive in their environments.

Adaptations

Animals live in many different places on Earth. An animal needs food, water, oxygen, and shelter. A trait that helps an animal meet its needs in the place where it lives is called an **adaptation.**

The webbed feet of a pelican are an adaptation. They help the pelican swim and survive in the water where it finds its food. Adaptations, such as webbed feet, are **inherited**, or passed on, from parents to their young.

Body parts, such as feet and bills, are important inherited adaptations. There are many different kinds of adaptations. Most kinds, such as body color, differ between members of even closely related groups.

This porcupine skull shows adaptations of a plant-eating animal. Sharp front teeth cut off parts of plants. Flat teeth in the back of the jaw move from side to side, grinding tough plant material.

This hyena skull shows adaptations of a meat-eating animal. Sharp front teeth tear off meat and back teeth shred it.

The bill of a pelican has a pouch that hangs from it. When a pelican swoops into the water for food, the pouch acts like a net to help the bird catch fish.

Adaptations for Getting Food

Animals have many special adaptations for getting food. Prairie dogs and moles have feet that are especially good for digging. Hawks and eagles have feet that can hold tightly onto their food when they swoop down to catch it. Animals may also have the kind of teeth that can handle the foods they eat. Many birds have bills that help them catch and eat their favorite foods. Sometimes you can tell what a bird eats by the shape of its bill.

A long, curved bill helps the flamingo filter food from shallow water.

A short, strong bill helps the cardinal break open seeds.

A small, thin bill helps the warbler pick out insects for food.

1. ✔**Checkpoint** Give two examples of adaptations and tell how they help the animal survive.

2. **Art** in Science Think about an animal that wades into ponds and spears fish for food. Draw a picture of this animal. Include the special adaptations you think it would need to live and get food.

Adaptations for Protection

The way an animal looks can help it survive. *Camouflage* helps some animals blend into their surroundings. Camouflage helps hide the animals from predators.

Other animals have colors or markings that copy those of a more dangerous animal. This kind of adaptation is called *mimicry.*

The way an animal acts can help it survive. Many animals climb, run, hop, jump, fly, or swim away from danger. Some animals may also use poison to protect themselves. Animals such as skunks and weasels spray a bad-smelling liquid at their enemies. Many animals use body parts such as shells, teeth, claws, hooves, and bills to protect themselves.

A porcupine is covered in quills. These special hairs have sharp hooks on their tips. When the porcupine is scared, special muscles make the quills stand up. Then the porcupine can hit an attacker with its quills. The hooks pierce the attacker's skin and stay attached to it.

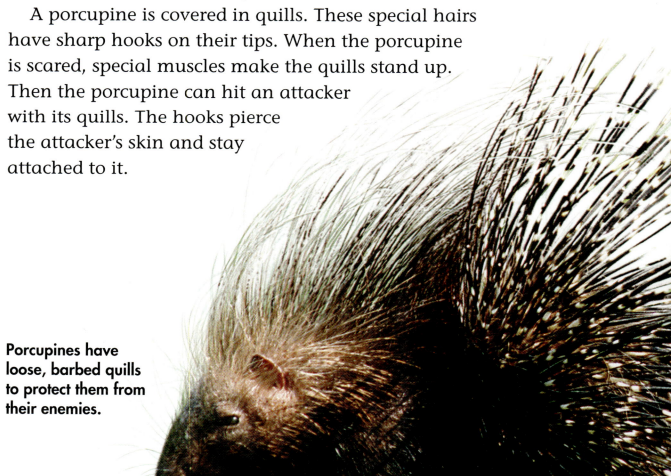

Porcupines have loose, barbed quills to protect them from their enemies.

Ways Animals Protect Themselves

Camouflage	Armor	Mimicry	Poison
Animals that can harm or be harmed by this crab spider cannot see it.	Spikes and horns protect this horned lizard.	A harmless hover fly looks like a dangerous hornet.	Lion fish have poisonous spines.
These harlequin shrimp blend in with the bright sea fans.	Pill bugs roll into a ball for defense.	A viceroy butterfly looks like a bad-tasting monarch butterfly.	Monarch butterflies taste bad because of the food they eat.
The fur color of this arctic fox changes with the seasons.	A cassowary has a tough helmet to protect its head as it runs through brush.	This king snake looks similar to the deadly coral snake.	Coral snakes bite with poisonous fangs.

1. ✓**Checkpoint**   What are some ways that animals protect themselves from their enemies?

2. 🎯 **Sequence** List in the correct sequence what happens when a predator attacks a porcupine. Be sure to use the signal words *first*, *next*, and *finally* in your list of steps.

51

Behaviors That Help Animals

Behaviors are things that animals do. Animals are born being able to do some things. These behaviors are inherited. You inherit your ability to do many things such as walk and talk.

You do not inherit your ability to read and write. You need to learn these behaviors. You do inherit your ability to learn these behaviors, though.

Baby birds are born knowing how to open their mouths for food.

Monarch butterflies have an instinct to migrate.

Instincts

An instinct is a behavior an animal is born able to do. One instinct is an animal's response to hunger. Baby birds, for example, open their mouths when they sense a parent with food is near. Some animals have an instinct to move, or **migrate,** when the seasons change. Some butterflies migrate thousands of miles to warmer weather to survive the winter.

Other animals have an instinct to **hibernate** during the cold winter months. When animals hibernate, their body systems usually slow down to save energy. Then they don't need as much food to survive.

Bats hibernate during the winter months when food is hard to find.

An adult chimp shows a young chimp how to dig for insects.

Learning

Animals learn some behaviors from their parents and other animals. For example, chimpanzees can learn how to use tools like sticks to catch insects to eat. Chimpanzees are not born knowing how to use sticks as tools. They learn how to do this by watching other chimpanzees. Young chimpanzees also learn which foods are safe to eat from their mothers and other adults.

Some young animals learn hunting behavior from their parents.

Lesson Checkpoint

1. Name two types of adaptations having to do with an animal's actions.

2. Why do some animals migrate or hibernate?

3. **Social Studies** in Science
Chimpanzees live in groups and learn how to behave from other chimpanzees. Describe how humans and chimpanzees are alike in the ways that they learn.

This trilobite fossil is a cast. It shows what the trilobite looked like.

A cast, such as this bird-like dinosaur, is in the shape of the original fossil. It formed when a mold was filled in with rock matter over time.

This fossil cast is of a dinosaur skull about 125 million years old! It looks like the skull of a modern-day crocodile.

How are animals from the past like today's animals?

Fossils show the kinds of animals that lived long ago. Today's animals are similar in some ways to animals of the past that have disappeared.

Animals That Lived Long Ago

Signs of past life are called fossils. Usually only the hard parts of animals become fossils. A fossil is usually not the actual bone or part. Instead, it is rock in the shape of the part.

A space in the shape of an animal in rock is called a fossil mold. Soft earth covers the remains of the animal, which wears away. This leaves a cavity or mold in the shape of the animal's parts. The earth then turns to rock over time. If the mold gets filled in with other rock materials over time, the fossil is called a cast.

Long ago, this spider got trapped in sticky tree sap that hardened into amber.

Unlike the fossil remains of most dinosaur bones, the bones of this fossil saber-toothed tiger are actual bone.

Ancient Insects

Some small animals, or parts of animals, have been found in hardened tree sap called amber. Long ago, an insect might have become trapped in the sticky sap. Soon the sap would have completely covered the insect. Over a long period of time, the sap turned into a hard, yellow or reddish-brown substance called amber. Thin pieces of amber are usually clear enough to see through. What you see is the animal's actual body covering kept together for millions of years.

One other type of fossil is found in tar pits. Saber-toothed tigers and other extinct animals fell into these oily pools many thousands of years ago. The soft parts of their bodies broke down and left only the bones. These fossils are the actual bones of these animals.

1. ✓**Checkpoint** What are some ways that fossils form?

2. **Math in Science** If a modern-day lizard is 10 meters long and a dinosaur skeleton is 3 times as long, how long is the dinosaur skeleton?

How Animals Today Compare to Those of Long Ago

Fossils can tell us how animals have changed over time. Dinosaurs are extinct. An extinct animal is a kind of animal that no longer lives on Earth. As you can see from the pictures, some animals today look like animals of long ago.

Fossils also tell us how Earth has changed over time. The drawing on the next page shows what the Badlands of South Dakota probably looked like more than 65 million years ago. At that time, dinosaurs like *Tyrannosaurus rex* roamed the area. Plant fossils found in layers of rocks near *T. rex* fossils tell scientists that the climate was hot and wet when *T. rex* lived. Plants could grow year-round. That is why you see plants in the drawing of the *T. rex*.

T. rex's habitat has changed a great deal. The photo in the drawing shows what the Badlands look like today. Only animals that are adapted to hot, dry conditions can live there now.

Although this collared lizard is a tiny, modern-day reptile, it resembles dinosaurs of long ago.

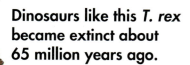

Dinosaurs like this *T. rex* became extinct about 65 million years ago.

Today the Badlands in South Dakota are almost like a desert.

This is one artist's view of how a T.rex might have looked. It also shows its habitat.

✓**Lesson Checkpoint**

1. Describe four kinds of fossils.

2. What can fossils tell us about extinct animals?

3. **Writing** in Science **Expository** In your **science journal,** write about what might have happened to *T. Rex* when its environment changed.

57

Investigate What can you learn from an imprint?

Imprint fossils are one type of fossil. Scientists can learn about animals that lived long ago by studying the imprints they made.

imprint made by a dinosaur

Materials

cup with prepared plaster of Paris

spoon

paper plate and paper towels

bowl of water

Process Skills

When you **observe** the imprint of your hand, you notice its size, shape, and texture.

What to Do

1 Put plaster of Paris onto a plate.

Spread the plaster of Paris around with a spoon.

2 Wet one of your hands.

Be careful!

Do not put plaster of Paris into a sink. It can clog the drain.

3 Spread the fingers of your wet hand. Press the palm side of this hand into the plaster of Paris.

4 Remove your hand from the plaster. Let the imprint dry.

Wipe the plaster of Paris off your hand. Use paper towels. Wash your hands thoroughly.

5 Make a chart to record what you **observe** about your hand and its imprint.

Appearance	
Imprint	**Hand**

Explain Your Results

1. How is your imprint like your hand that made it? How is it different?

2. **Infer** How might an imprint fossil of an animal be like the animal that made it? How might it be different?

Go Further

Use a hand lens to observe and study tiny details. If you wish, make sketches or diagrams. Use your ruler to measure your hand and its imprint.

Math in Science

Comparing Speeds of Fish

There is a great difference in the swimming speeds of fish. Generally, larger fish can swim faster than smaller fish. The bar graph below shows the greatest swimming speeds of six different fish.

Greatest Swimming Speeds

Fish (vertical axis): Barracuda, Southern Bluefin Tuna, Marlin, Salmon, Sailfish, Swordfish

Kilometers per hour (horizontal axis): 0, 5, 10, 15, 20, 25, 30, 35, 40, 45, 50, 55, 60, 65, 70, 75, 80, 85, 90, 95, 100, 105, 110

1 Which of the six fish is the fastest swimmer?

    A. Salmon   B. Marlin

    C. Barracuda   D. Sailfish

2 Which of the six fish is the slowest swimmer?

    F. Swordfish   G. Barracuda

    H. Southern Bluefin Tuna   I. Marlin

3 Use the data in the graph to list the six fish in order from slowest to fastest.

Lab zone **Take-Home Activity**

Use an almanac, the Internet, or other sources to find the most recent Olympic records for swimming. Make a graph or a chart showing the record times for each swimming event.

61

Use Vocabulary

adaptation (page 48)	**migrate** (page 52)
hibernate (page 52)	**pupa** (page 45)
	trait (page 40)
inherited (page 48)	**vertebrate** (page 40)
larva (page 45)	

Use the vocabulary word from the list above that best completes each sentence.

1. An animal with a backbone is called a(n) _____.

2. In an early stage of life, when a butterfly eats and grows, it is called a(n) _____.

3. Some animals need much less food to survive when they _____.

4. Something that helps a living thing survive is called a(n) _____.

5. If something passes on from a parent to its offspring, it is _____.

6. The stage in the life cycle of a butterfly during which it changes into an adult is called the _____.

7. Sometimes animals move to another place, or _____, to find better food or shelter.

8. A feature passed on to an animal from its parents is a(n) _____.

Explain Concepts

9. Explain why different animals can be grouped in more than one way.

10. Why does inheriting an adaptation help offspring survive?

11. What is the difference between instinct and learned behavior?

12. Describe the changes a frog goes through during its life cycle.

Process Skills

13. **Infer** If a fossil skull has flat teeth, what do you think this animal probably ate?

14. **Predict** A hawk has feet with sharp claws on them to help it catch small animals to eat. What kind of feet would you predict a bird that swims would have?

MindPoint Quiz Show

Sequence

15. Use the signal words to put the stages of the life cycle of a frog in the correct sequence.

First

↓

Next

↓

Finally

Test Prep

Choose the letter that best completes the statement or answers the question.

16. Fossils tell us
- Ⓐ about animals that lived in the past.
- Ⓑ about how Earth has changed.
- Ⓒ how today's animals are similar to past life.
- Ⓓ all of the above.

17. The earliest stage in a frog's life cycle is a(n)
- Ⓕ pupa.
- Ⓖ egg.
- Ⓗ chrysalis.
- Ⓘ tadpole.

18. Which of the following is an animal without a backbone, or invertebrate?
- Ⓐ insect
- Ⓑ bird
- Ⓒ mammal
- Ⓓ amphibian

19. Explain why the answer you chose for Question 18 is best. For each of the answers you did not choose, give a reason why it is not the correct choice.

20. **Writing** in Science

Descriptive Suppose a hungry fox comes upon a porcupine. Write a paragraph describing what happens between the two animals.

Paul Sereno:
Expert Dinosaur Hunter

Paul Sereno

When he was a boy, Paul Sereno liked to go on nature hikes with his brothers. He brought home insects to add to his collection. Paul went to college to study art. However, while he was in college, Paul decided he wanted to become a paleontologist—a scientist who studies ancient life.

Paleontologists like Dr. Sereno try to find fossils to piece together the story of what life was like long ago. Dr. Sereno and his team have found many new kinds of dinosaurs.

Dr. Sereno's team made a discovery in Africa. A giant claw lying in the desert was the first clue. Dr. Sereno and his team carefully dug for more bones. They found a huge skeleton of a dinosaur. Its skull was long with crocodile-like teeth. Dr. Sereno named the new dinosaur *Suchomimus* which means "crocodile mimic."

It sometimes takes years for paleontologists to make sense of what they find. But their hard work often leads to new discoveries.

Lab zone Take-Home Activity

Using library resources and the Internet, research newly discovered dinosaurs. List them by name, type of dinosaur, and where found.